So You're
50!

Mike Haskins & Clive Whichelow

SO YOU'RE 50!

Summersdale Publishers Ltd
46 West Street
Chichester
West Sussex
PO19 1RP
UK

www.summersdale.com

Printed and bound by Tien Wah Press, Singapore

ISBN 13: 978-1-84024-563-9

So You're

50!

Mike Haskins & Clive Whichelow

INTRODUCTION

So you've done it! You've reached another of life's milestones. You've reached the age you never thought you'd reach. And it isn't even the first age you never thought you'd reach that you've reached. It's probably something like the third or fourth.

And here it is. The big one: 50. It's a wonder the shock of it hasn't killed you. Especially at your age.

More to the point, how are you going to cope with the fact that every time you tell someone your age, they will start whistling the theme tune from *Hawaii Five-O*?

If, that is, they're old enough to remember it.

And you can't argue with people who call you middle-aged any more. Oh yes, you tried to deny it throughout your decade as a giddy young 40-something. But in your 50s, you have no defence.

Thankfully, this little volume will help you adjust. Sit awhile, relax and ponder on the many rich mysteries with which life has presented you.

Such as why, when you have spent every last hard-earned penny raising and educating your kids and imparted your worldly wisdom to them, they have grown up into people with whom you have nothing in common whatsoever?

Well, we can ponder these things, but there probably aren't any answers.

THE BASIC MYTHS ABOUT TURNING 50

50 is the new 40. It's not.

You'll be older and wiser –
older and wider maybe.

Saga holidays are the new 18 to 30
– no they're not, but they do involve
going on holiday with a bunch of people
who look like they were born in 1830.

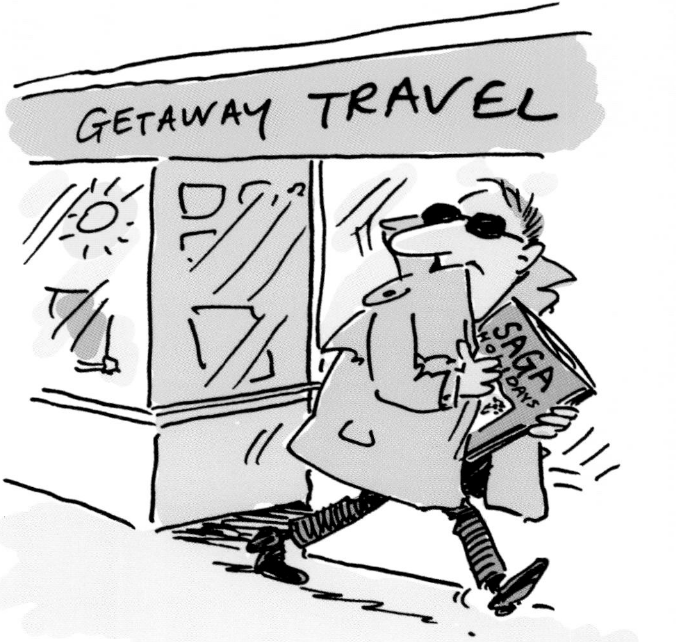
GETAWAY TRAVEL
SAGA

Soon your kids will have flown the coop – don't fool yourself. Your kids are flying nowhere. Apart from off to Ibiza for a fortnight at your expense.

THINGS YOU WILL NEVER NOW DO

Be a *Playboy/Playgirl* centrefold – unless the criteria for the job changes drastically

Be Young Businessperson of the Year

Learn to dance in a way that doesn't embarrass your children

DRESS CODE FOR THE OVER 50s – SOME DO'S & DON'TS

Don't try to look younger by body piercing – it will just look like you had a really horrible accident while doing some DIY.

Do cover up your midriff or it will look
like you're carrying an airbag
made of lard.

Don't dress in a track suit and bling as
you will now look less like a bad ass
rapper and more like Jimmy Savile.

Don't even think about a thong –
remember Peter Stringfellow?!

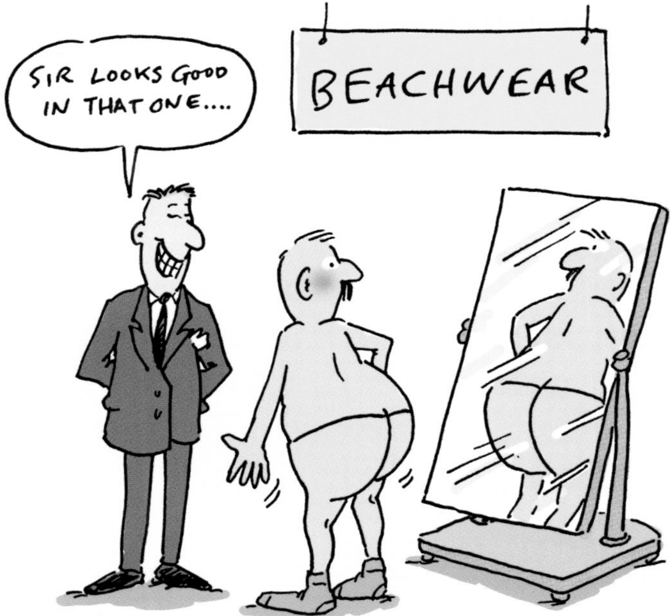
SIR LOOKS GOOD IN THAT ONE....
BEACHWEAR

CULTURE CONVERTER

When speaking with people younger than yourself it's no use talking about things that happened before they were born, they won't have a clue what you're on about. So here is a handy culture converter to translate your cultural reference points to their equivalent:

Category	Your Age	People Younger Than You But Scarily Classed as Middle-aged	Even Younger People	Indisputably Young People
Transport	Chopper bike	Skateboard	Roller blades	Hot-wired Ford Fiesta
Must-have electronic gadget	Calculator	Digital watch	Sony Walkman	All-in-one TV, computer, MP3, phone, camera
Sweeties	Spangles	Opal Fruits	Skittles	Ecstasy
Means of communicating with friends	Tin cans with string between them	Invisible ink	CB radio	E-mail, mobile phones, text messages, MSN
Embarrassing teenage pop hero	Gary Glitter	Adam Ant	Shakin' Stevens	Marilyn Manson

HOW TO APPEAR YOUNGER
THAN YOU ACTUALLY ARE

Wear your baseball cap back to front.

Swap the car for a moped
with an L-plate.

Do not wear your glasses on a little necklace
round your neck – not only do they make
you look ancient, they tell the world that you
are so absent-minded you will forget in an
instant where you've left your glasses.

Hang around with people even older than you are (e.g. if possible join the Rolling Stones).

Learn to sit down without saying 'Aah, that's better'.

A GUIDE TO HOW OTHERS WILL NOW PERCEIVE YOU

A reactionary old git

Someone who is now unemployable

Someone who knows nothing
about computers

A health insurance risk

In need of plastic surgery

THE MAIN EVENTS IN YOUR LIFE YOU CAN NOW LOOK FORWARD TO

Having a beautiful set of white
teeth which are not only all new but
removable for easy cleaning

A second honeymoon – and being able
to get out to see the sights this time

Saving money on your central heating
as a result of having hot flushes

THE MAIN EVENTS IN YOUR LIFE IT'S LESS EASY TO LOOK FORWARD TO

Becoming a grandparent before you're mentally attuned to the idea

Losing brain cells – then again if you lose enough, you won't notice

The first time you get out of breath
running up the stairs

Having progressively less hair to
comb and more face to wash

CONVERSING WITH YOUNG PEOPLE (PART 1)

What you say and what they hear

'How are you getting on at university?'
= 'Are you on drugs?'

'Have you got a boyfriend/girlfriend
yet?' = 'Are you gay?'

'We didn't use to bother with sell-by dates in my day.' = 'Scrape the mould off the bread and stop whinging.'

'In my day you could have a wonderful night out and still have change from ten bob.' = 'I am an old skinflint now and always have been.'

STATISTICALLY SPEAKING

OK. Now the bad news.

If you're exactly 50 years old this means you have been alive for 18,262 days.

50 years is also 438,288 hours, 26,297,280 minutes or 1,577,836,800 seconds.

Telling people you have lived for a period of well over one and a half billion anythings is probably going to make you sound quite old.

At an average heart rate of 72 beats a minute, your heart has now beaten around 1,893,404,160 times. So no wonder you feel tired.

OK, probably around half a billion of those beats happened when you were running round the house trying to find your passport before going on holiday last year.

Taking twelve breaths per minute at an average of 0.5 litres of air per breath means 157,783,680 litres of the air currently in the earth's atmosphere have been inside you at some point. So I hope you've been using breath freshener.

NOW YOU'RE 50 THE FOLLOWING WILL BE YOUR NATURAL ENEMIES

Patronising sales assistants in clothes shops

Bathroom scales

The people who make it impossible
to open plastic bottle tops

The people who write instruction
manuals for new-fangled electrical
items and self-assembly furniture

A LIST OF CONTROVERSIAL OPINIONS YOU WILL NOW BE EXPECTED TO HOLD

'Not only does capital punishment have a lot going for it, it should be introduced for all motoring offences.'

'Being unemployed should be against
the law – and therefore subject
to capital punishment.'

'There have been no decent records
made since 1979.'

CONVERSING WITH YOUNG PEOPLE (PART 2)

What they say and what you hear

'Is it all right if I stay over with a friend tonight?' = 'I am going to an orgy.'

'I'm moving out and getting a place of my own.' = 'I'll be back Saturday.'

'I know I've been out with a few people, but I think this latest one really is the one.' = 'I have finally lost all judgement when it comes to the opposite sex.'

'I'm thinking of getting married.' = 'There's a baby on the way.'

THINGS YOU CAN NOW GET AWAY WITH THAT YOU COULDN'T PREVIOUSLY

Admitting to yourself you are and have always been a right-wing reactionary who deep down doesn't actually like anybody that much

Being obsessed with gardening

Buying £3 supermarket jeans – and maybe even wearing them

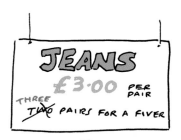

THINGS YOU SHOULD HAVE ACHIEVED BY NOW

Being able to walk along the pavement
without dodging the cracks

Being able to talk to your bank
manager as an equal

Being able to sustain the same hairstyle
you've had for the past thirty years
regardless of prevailing fashion and/or
how much hair you have left

THINGS YOU ARE NOW LIKELY TO HAVE IN YOUR HOME

A Neighbourhood Watch sticker in your window

A smoke alarm that actually works – particularly when you make toast

A box in the attic full of pictures painted
by your children when they
were young and nice

Proper framed pictures
(posters don't count!)

THINGS THAT YOU WILL TAKE A SUDDEN INTEREST IN

Pension annuity levels

Newspaper articles on heart attack warning signs

Other peoples' operations

THINGS YOU'LL FEEL SMUG ABOUT

Being better at grammar than a 20 year-old with an English degree

Going up the stairs rather than taking the lift

The neatness of your front garden

HOORAY! THINGS YOU'LL NEVER HAVE TO DO AGAIN

Change a nappy – until the grandchildren arrive that is

Be treated as nothing more than a sex object

Explain how babies are made

BOO! THINGS YOU WON'T BE DOING AGAIN

Having a wide choice of hairstyles

Painting a white stripe down the side of your Ford Cortina to make yourself look like Starsky and Hutch

Being asked to turn the noise down

Being treated as nothing more
than a sex object

SHATTERING MOMENTS TO COME SOON

Your first pair of bifocals

When you wake up with a terrible hangover and remember you didn't have a drink the night before

Walking down the high street seeing an individual who is clearly mutton dressed as lamb only to then realise it's your own reflection in a shop window

Realising if you're now given a life prison sentence, it might actually mean life

THINGS TO EXPECT FOR YOUR NEXT BIRTHDAY

A specially arranged surprise reunion with people you hoped never to see again

A tin of biscuits in a little pack with a small jar of strawberry jam

Enough socks to last you the rest of your life

GADGETS THAT ONLY THE OVER 50s WILL REMEMBER

Dansette autochange record players

Bubble cars

Televisions with wooden doors to open
and close across the screen

Anything made by K-tel or Ronco

BEING 50 IS...

... being too old for basketball but too young for bowls.

... being too old for cruising but too young for a cruise.

...being too old for a trendy haircut but too young for a hairpiece.

AARGHH! THINGS YOU NEVER THOUGHT WOULD HAPPEN

If you want a head rush all you have to do is stand up too quickly.

Your 'comfort-fit' jeans are too tight.

You fancy afternoon TV presenters.

If you are a man you can at last
see a pair of beautifully developed
naked breasts any time you want
– unfortunately they're yours.

YOUR NEW OUTLOOK ON LIFE

Your idea of a sensual massage is
provided by one of those big vibrating
blue sock things you stick your feet in
and plug into the mains.

Your idea of a dirty weekend is clearing out the garden shed.

Your idea of a wild night is not going to bed straight after the *Ten O'clock News.*

YOUR NEW WEEKLY HIGHLIGHTS

Having a chat with the milkman

The local newspaper printing your latest letter complaining about something

For ladies the weekly exercise work-out in the church hall, for men walking past and peering through the window of the church hall while the ladies' weekly exercise work-out is in full swing

THINGS YOU WILL DESPERATELY TRY TO AVOID

Viagra (in public at least)

Long-johns

For men the comb over, for the ladies
expandable waist trousers

THINGS YOU SHOULD NOT HAVE IN YOUR CAR

Tinted windows – for boy racers only

A tin of sweets and a box of tissues
– you're not quite that old yet

'Baby on board' sticker
– you're fooling no one!

THINGS YOU WON'T BE DOING ON HOLIDAY ANY MORE

Having a run-in with the local police

Getting chatted up by the waiter/waitress

Hiring a moped without a crash helmet

Running out of money on day three

REASONS TO BE CHEERFUL

You're now old enough to
have a toy boy/girl

You're still much younger than Harrison Ford or Glenn Close

In a hostage situation you are likely to be released first

www.summersdale.com